MOVIEMAKERS' FILM CLUB

Be a
SOUND DESIGNER

Creating a MOOD

PowerKiDS press

by
Alix Wood

Published in 2018 by Rosen Publishing
29 East 21st Street, New York, NY 10010

CATALOGING-IN-PUBLICATION DATA

Names: Wood, Alix.
Title: Be a sound designer: creating a mood / Alix Wood.
Description: New York : PowerKids Press, 2018. | Series: Moviemakers' film club | Includes
index.
Identifiers: LCCN ISBN 9781538323809 (pbk.) | ISBN 9781508162575 (library bound) | ISBN
9781538323816 (6 pack)
Subjects: LCSH: Sound motion pictures--Juvenile literature. | Sound--Recording and
reproducing--Juvenile literature. | Motion pictures--Sound effects--Juvenile literature.
Classification: LCC PN1995.7 W64 2018 | DDC 791.43--dc23

Produced for Rosen Publishing by Alix Wood Books
Designed by Alix Wood
Editor: Eloise Macgregor
Editor for Rosen: Kerri O'Donnell
Series consultant: Cameron Browne

Photo credits: Cover, 1, 4, 5, 6, 7, 8, 9, 10, 11, 13, 14, 15 bottom, 17, 18, 19, 20, 22, 23, 25,
27, 28, 29 © Adobe Stock Images; 12 © Jonathan Moran; 15 top, 16, 21 © Cameron Browne;
24 © Vancouver Film School

Printed in the United States of America

CPSIA compliance information: Batch # BW18PK: For further information contact
Rosen Publishing, New York, New York at 1-800-542-2595.

CONTENTS

INTRODUCING THE
SOUND DESIGNER!

Driving into the city, you see a railroad yard up ahead. The trains are making a loud clanking sound as they move up and down the rails. You can hear a metal scraping noise as the brakes start to bite on the wheels. This is amazing! You jump out of your car and grab your sound recording gear from the trunk. This has made your day!

Sound designers are always on the lookout for new sounds. When you watch a movie, you may not really think about what you are hearing. Obviously it is important to be able to hear what the characters are saying, but what do sound designers do for the rest of the movie? The answer is "Plenty!" Every tiny sound, every piece of music, every monster's roar has been found or created by the sound designer.

Great sounds are everywhere once you start to tune in!

A sound designer has to...

- Love sound and the movies
- Have knowledge of the science of sound, or **acoustics**
- Understand sound recording and editing techniques
- Have excellent listening skills

- Be creative
- Be a good communicator
- Be able to work to deadlines
- Be organized
- Understand how to stay safe while working on set

Cell Phone Movie School

Try watching an action scene with the sound turned down. Then turn the volume back up again and you will understand what a sound designer's job involves. The music, the sound effects, and the background noise all help to give the scene its drama and its setting.

"The most important thing you can do as a sound designer is to make the right choice for the right sound at the right moment..."

Ben Burtt

SOUND EQUIPMENT

When you first start out recording sound you won't want to spend much money on equipment. You can use the built-in microphone on your smartphone or camera, at first.

Cell Phone Movie School

A smartphone is a good, cheap, and portable way to record sound. The main problem with using a smartphone or a "point-and-shoot" camera's built-in microphone is that it is in your hand, and not near the source of the sound. As you move your camera around to get different shots, the sound will change. It also picks up other unwanted sounds, such as road traffic. You can get a much better sound recording if you use a separate microphone placed near the sound that you are recording.

Lavalier microphones (or "tie clip" mics) are worn on clothes or taped to the body. They are a good way to record voices. Some have to be attached to the camera by a cable, but others are wireless.

Shotgun microphones are directional. That means they mainly pick up sound from directly in front of them. This helps cut out any background noise. They are often held over the head of the person who is speaking using a long pole known as a **boom**.

Do I Need Headphones?

It helps to wear headphones when you are recording. Headphones help you listen to what your microphone is picking up. It is surprising how much background noise you can miss if you don't wear headphones. Most cameras have a headphone socket. Smartphones may need a headphone **adaptor**.

You can always make your own boom. Simply duct-tape your microphone to a hockey stick, broom handle, or long paint roller!

As you progress, you may want to use some special tools to mix your **soundtrack** together. There are some smartphone apps available, or you can use **software** on a computer.

GETTING YOUR EARS TUNED IN

To be a great sound designer you need to have what they call a "good ear." How do you get a good ear? Some people can naturally hear the differences in sounds better than others, but you can train your ears. Look for free online ear trainer programs that may help you improve your listening skills.

Look after your ears. Get them checked regularly. Don't damage your ears by listening to your music too loud.

Have You Got Golden Ears?

Try this test. Close all the doors and windows in a room. Now clap your hands. You should hear four distinct sounds:

- The sound of the hands coming together is known as the **attack**.
- The **body** is where the sound intensifies and is at its loudest.
- The sound then bounces off the walls and other surfaces and returns to your ears, known as the **echo**.
- The sound fading away to nothing is called the **decay**.

Try tuning your ear so you can hear each of these sounds.

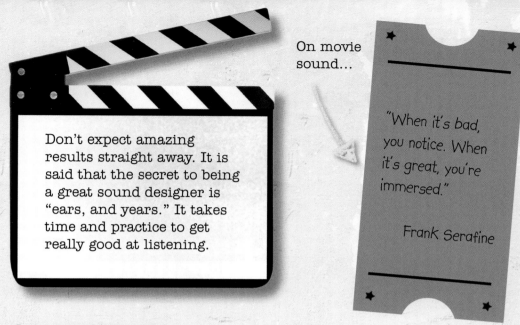

Don't expect amazing results straight away. It is said that the secret to being a great sound designer is "ears, and years." It takes time and practice to get really good at listening.

On movie sound...

"When it's bad, you notice. When it's great, you're immersed."

Frank Serafine

Learn to Listen

Ask a friend to choose a movie DVD, without you knowing which one they chose. Close your eyes or wear a blindfold. Then ask them to play you a clip from the movie. Focus on the sound. Once the clip has finished, write down what sounds you heard, what might have made them, and what you think was happening in the movie. Now watch the same clip. Were you right? Are there any sounds you missed?

Now watch another clip with the sound off. Can you predict what kind of music might be playing over the clip? Try to choose a piece of music that would suit the scene.

UNDERSTANDING SOUND

A sound designer needs to understand how sound works. Sound waves are produced by **vibrations**, such as the tiny movements that a guitar string makes when you pluck it. These vibrations travel through **molecules** in the air. Each vibrating molecule will cause the molecule next to it to vibrate, allowing the sound to travel.

Dealing With Echoes

Some surfaces make a sound echo. The sound bounces off the surfaces and seems to repeat itself around the space. A room with hard, smooth surfaces, such as a tiled bathroom, will produce echoes. Empty rooms often produce an echo, too. Rough surfaces absorb sound. Carpet, wood paneling, and soft furniture like in the room below would all help soften any echoes.

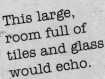

This large, room full of tiles and glass would echo.

Playing With Sound Waves

Sound-mixing software translates the vibrations a sound wave makes into an image that you can see on screen. Sound designers use these images and other information the software gives them to examine their soundtrack. They then decide which sounds need to be louder or quieter. They can edit the soundtrack by chopping bits out, moving parts around, or adding pieces in.

Cell Phone Movie School

Some sounds are actually too low for us to be able to hear them. Sound can be felt as well as heard. A good movie theater sound system can make the room rumble when playing really low sounds.

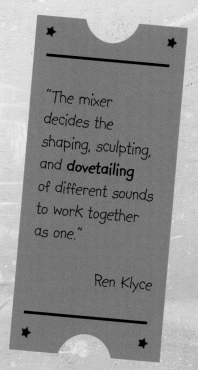

"The mixer decides the shaping, sculpting, and **dovetailing** of different sounds to work together as one."

Ren Klyce

WORKING ON SET

The sound crew usually arrives on set half an hour before filming starts. They have to unload their truck and set up their equipment. During the rehearsals the **director**, **director of photography**, **sound mixer**, and **boom operator** get together with the actors to plan camera moves, lighting, and sound. The sound team plans where to put their microphones. They need to make sure their microphones won't annoy the camera crew by getting in the shot or casting shadows, too.

Who Does What On Set

Sound Mixer - sits just off set and checks to make sure any recorded **dialogue** is clear.

Boom Operator - responsible for positioning the microphones, and keeping the boom mic out of the shot.

Sound Assistant - checks and helps move the equipment, keeps the batteries charged, and investigates and stops any unwanted noises.

Sound Trainee - on a busy set, a sound department may have a trainee who helps move equipment and run errands.

A production sound mixer at work

A slate or clapboard helps the film editor **synchronize** the sound with the picture. The sound of the clap and the image of the same clap can be matched up so the sound and picture run perfectly together.

The Assistant director will usually run the set. Commands at the beginning of each take usually follow this order.

Assistant director: "Quiet on the set."

Assistant director: "Roll sound."

Sound mixer: "Rolling."

Camera assistant: "Scene one, take one."

Assistant director: "Roll camera."

Camera operator: "Rolling."

Camera assistant: "Marker" (then claps using the slate).

Camera operator: "Camera set."

Director: "Action."

Cell Phone Movie School

If you forget your clapboard, or don't have one, try this trick instead. Ask an actor or one of the crew to look into the camera, say the take or scene number, and hold up that many fingers. Then ask them to clap. As long as you don't go past ten takes and the person runs out of fingers, this can work as well as a clapboard.

RECORDING OUTSIDE

Recording sound outside can be difficult. Background noises might easily interrupt your filming. A plane may fly overhead, birds can start chirping, a neighbor might fire up their lawn mower. Weather can mess up your sound recording, too.

"The most important skill for any sound designer to have is willpower. Never give up."

Charles Deenen

Scout Out Your Location

Visit **locations** before you start filming to check for any problems, such as:
- traffic noise, planes, and trains
- nature sounds
- noise from factories or building sites
- air conditioning units
- strong winds

If the place you had in mind has too many of these things, find a different location.

Blocking Unwanted Sounds

Actors wearing lavalier microphones can stand with their back to the noise. Their body will help block the sound. Buildings, rocks, and trees will also help block sound. A carefully placed shotgun microphone should just pick up the sound you want, too.

What problems might these young filmmakers find when recording sound in this location? Leaves rustling? Twigs snapping? Birds chirping? Dogs barking?

Cell Phone Movie School

Wind noise can badly interfere with your sound recording. Sound recordists cover their microphones with windshields made of foam or fur. The furry type of windshield pictured below is known as a "dead cat"! It works by creating a dead air space around the microphone, protecting it from moving air. You can make your own dead cat by wrapping fiber batting from a quilt around the microphone and securing it in place using rubber bands. Then place a layer of fake fur on the top and secure it in the same way. You can also make a windshield by putting your microphone inside an upturned mesh laundry basket, and securing it in place with rubber bands.

RECORDING INDOORS

Shooting film indoors has its own problems. When choosing your location, make sure the room is large enough. You will need space for the actors and all the crew to work in. The person holding the boom will need enough space so they can be out of camera shot.

Try not to select an empty room as a location. Empty rooms echo. Carpets and soft furniture help absorb sound. If you have to use an empty room, fill it with things like cushions, sleeping bags, and blankets. Spread a blanket on the floor and hang blankets on the walls on either side of the actors, out of camera shot.

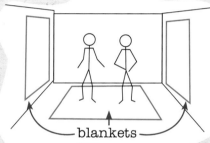

blankets

Room Tone

Once you have your room as you want it, remember to record around 30 seconds of **room tone**. Room tone is what the room sounds like when it is quiet. No room is ever actually completely silent. The "silence" will be different for every location. When you edit your sound later you can use your room tone as a background for any sound effects or to fill any gaps.

On set, the sound team will meet with the director and the director of photography to work out the camera movements for the scene. This process is called "blocking the action." It is important to work out how not to get in each other's way when working in a tight space.

Prepping the Set

Once you have discussed the day's filming with the director you will want to set up your microphones. To make sure lavalier mics stay in place, tape them to the actor's body using hairpiece tape.

Prepare any other mics and boom poles you may need. You may want to use a plant microphone, too. A plant is a microphone placed in a hidden spot, such as in a plant or a vase of flowers.

Cell Phone Movie School

A simple way to get better sound is to put up a "Quiet please" sign!

Quiet please
Filming in progress

Sound Check

Once you are set up, ask an actor or crew member to say a few lines so you can check your equipment is working. Listen to the playback using headphones to make sure you don't have any unwanted sounds in your room. Then you are ready for action!

GETTING THE DIALOGUE

Action! The actors start to walk along the beach, saying their lines. The cameraman is walking backwards filming, guided by a **grip** so he doesn't trip over anything. Your boom operator tries to hold the microphone steady over the actors' heads as they walk. You grab his coat and guide him backwards while he tries to stay out of shot, but still be close enough to get a good recording. A sound designer's job is not a simple one!

How To Hold a Boom

- Point the mic down, roughly over the actor's head.
- Hold the boom as level to the ground as you can.
- Stay out of shot.
- To record two actors' dialogue at once, hold the boom between them and then turn it so the mic points at whichever actor is speaking.
- Make the pole longer than you need. Holding it closer to the middle is easier than holding the end.

Always try to get the best sound you can while filming on location. You might re-record some of the dialogue with the actors in the studio later, but it is always better to have a soundtrack to match that to, even if it is a little rough.

It also makes life easier later if you can record each actor's dialogue separately. Using lavalier microphones is the best way to do this. Then you will be able to edit each character's soundtrack individually.

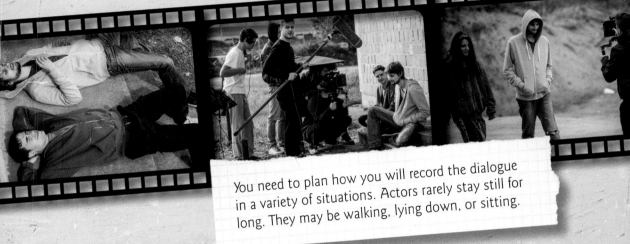

You need to plan how you will record the dialogue in a variety of situations. Actors rarely stay still for long. They may be walking, lying down, or sitting.

Cell Phone Movie School

When recording speech, saying letters such as P and B can sound bad. We tend to breathe out a blast of air when saying these letters, which sound even worse when recorded. Sound designers use a **pop shield** to help. A pop shield is a mesh screen placed in front of the microphone. You can make your own pop shield by wrapping a thin sock or a nylon stocking around a wire coat hanger.

VOICE-OVERS AND ADR

No matter how hard you try, sometimes your recorded dialogue may not be good enough for the final movie. That is where audio dialogue replacement (**ADR**) comes in. The sound department re-records dialogue, using the original actor, to improve the sound or make script changes.

ADR is usually recorded in a specialized sound studio. The actor watches the scene, listening to the sound that was recorded on location. The actor then recreates the performance word for word. This is why you must always make a location sound track, known as a scratch track. The scratch track acts as a guide to help the actor match his original dialogue to the recording.

An actor recording ADR. The microphone is fitted with a pop shield.

When Is ADR Used?

- To improve how a line was delivered
- When a line of dialogue has been changed
- To improve the timing
- To record a better singing voice than the actor had
- To remove unwanted background noise

Cell Phone Movie School

To decide if your film needs any ADR, have a spotting session with your team to discuss any sound issues. Check the dialogue for any problems. Has the actor mispronounced a word? Has their accent changed during the scene? Sometimes sound can be replaced using recorded dialogue from elsewhere in the movie. If this is not possible, then ADR is used. It is usually best to replace the dialogue for a whole scene so the background room tone all matches.

Voice-overs

A voice-over is where a character who is not on screen at the time talks over the images being shown. The technique is often used when a character talks about past events. A voice over might be done by a character not even in the story, but who has extra information about the events. Voice-overs are recorded after filming, in a studio.

Voice-matching is a very special kind of ADR. Voice matching actors match the voice of well-known actors. They do the ADR instead of the actual actor, who might be busy, hate doing ADR, or occasionally may even have died.

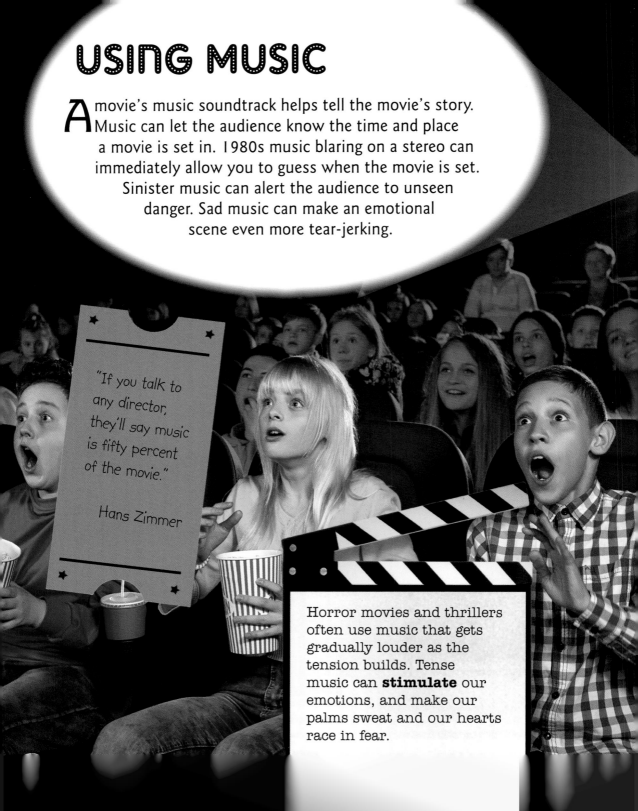

USING MUSIC

A movie's music soundtrack helps tell the movie's story. Music can let the audience know the time and place a movie is set in. 1980s music blaring on a stereo can immediately allow you to guess when the movie is set. Sinister music can alert the audience to unseen danger. Sad music can make an emotional scene even more tear-jerking.

"If you talk to any director, they'll say music is fifty percent of the movie."

Hans Zimmer

Horror movies and thrillers often use music that gets gradually louder as the tension builds. Tense music can **stimulate** our emotions, and make our palms sweat and our hearts race in fear.

Sometimes a sound designer might create a musical theme tune for a character. Darth Vader from the *Star Wars* movies had a chilling tune that was often played when he was on-screen.

Music can subtly let the viewer know that all is not as it seems. Sinister music playing while a character is doing something ordinary, like riding a bike, makes the audience start to suspect that something is not quite right.

Look at these movie stills. Try creating a mood for them by playing some magical music, then some scary music, and then some happy music. Which one suits the scene the best, do you think?

Cell Phone Movie School

Always make sure you are allowed to use any music you download. You can buy **royalty-free** soundtracks. You pay a fee to be allowed to use them. If you have any musical talent, it is cheaper to make your own movie soundtrack.

SOUND EFFECTS

Part of the job of a sound designer is to organize any sound effects. Many movie sounds are added after filming, during **post-production**. Sound recordists on set try to avoid picking up noises such as doors slamming or doorbells ringing. Why? By adding them later, the sound designer has complete control over their timing, quality, and how loud they are.

Some post-production sound effects are known as **Foley effects**. Foley effects are done in a sound studio by Foley artists who specialize in making sounds for film and TV. They might record footsteps on different surfaces such as marble, gravel, or piles of rock. They also create the sounds made when a character moves, such as material swishing together as an actor crosses their legs.

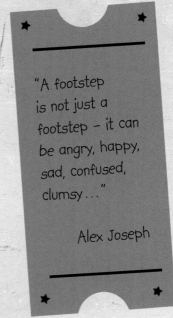

"A footstep is not just a footstep – it can be angry, happy, sad, confused, clumsy…"

Alex Joseph

This Foley artist is recording footsteps. He watches the scene on a screen to get the timing of the steps right.

Cell Phone Movie School

Make your own sound studio. Choose a quiet room away from any other noise. Gather some of the items below and try recording your own cool sound effects.

- Squeezing cornstarch in a cloth sounds like snow crunching.
- Flapping a pair of gloves sounds like a bird flying.
- Waving a thin stick makes a whooshing sound.
- Gelatin mixed with hand soap is good for squishing noises.

- Hit a couch with a broom or mop for a punch noise.
- Coconut shell halves stuffed with padding make hoof noises.
- Cellophane creates crackling fire effects.
- A can of dog food can be used for squelching noises.

Don't have time to record leaves rustling? There are libraries of prerecorded sound effects that you can drag and drop into your soundtrack. Even the pros use them. Ask an adult to help you, as downloads can sometimes contain nasty computer viruses.

SOUND EDITING

Once you have recorded your dialogue and created your sound effects, it's time to put it all together. Sound designers use sound editing software to create the final soundtrack for their movie.

Post-production sound mixing usually has three stages. First, mixers take the existing dialogue recorded on set and tidy it up. Then they add all the sound effects, Foley, background atmosphere noises, and replace any poor dialogue with ADR. The final stage involves mixing all those tracks into the **final mix**.

Cell Phone Movie School

Don't have expensive sound mixing equipment? No problem. There are some free smartphone apps, such as Splice, that you can use to edit your soundtrack. Other software, such as iMovie, is not too expensive. Most of these apps will allow you to edit sound, and add voice-overs and music. Some software allows you to edit multiple sound tracks.

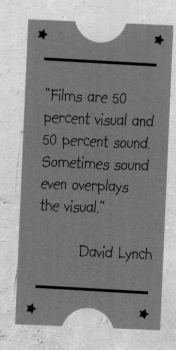

"Films are 50 percent visual and 50 percent sound. Sometimes sound even overplays the visual."

David Lynch

Sound vibrations usually appear as waves on screen. Mixing programs let you play with those waves and alter the sound. Learn how your mixing program works. Watch any tutorials that you can find. Then have fun and experiment.

You can make sound effects using editing software. If your program has a delay filter, try repeating some dialogue with a delay. Adjusting the delay can make it sound as if two people are speaking, or sound like a robotic voice, or an echo. Speeding dialogue up makes voices sound high-pitched, slowing speech down makes voices sound much deeper.

Post-production Tricks

- **Equalizers** can change the character of the sound, making it deeper or higher, and can help fix problems in the recording.
- Filters can get rid of background noise, such as hums and wind noise.
- Dropping the volume of background music helps make the dialogue or voice-over easier to hear.
- A little more **bass** added to the dialogue makes it sound more powerful, but not too much or it will sound muddy.
- Turning up the **sibilance** can make a recording clearer. Turn down the sibilance if there are too many harsh "s" sounds.
- Make sure different sounds are in different frequency ranges, so they don't overlap or cancel each other out. Dialogue should be in the middle of the frequency range.

MAKING YOUR NAME

To get yourself noticed, you need to make a **showreel** to show people your talents. A showreel contains examples of the best bits of work that you have done. So, how do you make a whole bunch of sounds stand out from the crowd?

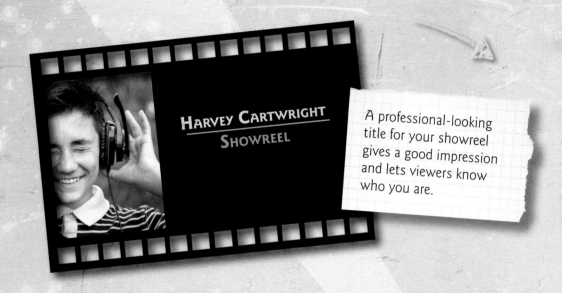

HARVEY CARTWRIGHT
SHOWREEL

A professional-looking title for your showreel gives a good impression and lets viewers know who you are.

Tell a Story

See if you can link together some of your best sound effects and recorded dialogue to make a story. Being able to tell a story using sound is the heart of what makes a great sound designer.

Borrow Footage

Images help bring a showreel to life. Try adding a soundtrack to a real movie trailer. Make sure you state that you have "borrowed" the images and credit the original movie in your showreel.

How To Impress

It is not just your work that will impress people on set. Here are some tips on movie set manners that will help you fit in.

- Be polite.

- Remember people's names.

- Always be cheerful and pleasant. No one wants to work with a grumpy person.

- If you ever have to walk in front of a camera lens, or a light that might cast a shadow, say "Crossing!" to warn the camera operator.

- Always ask people first if you need to move their equipment out of the way.

- Never interfere with other departments' jobs, just do your job.

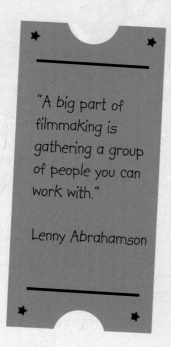

"A big part of filmmaking is gathering a group of people you can work with."

Lenny Abrahamson

Cell Phone Movie School

It's not always easy to get experience as a sound designer. Try offering to work on student or community film projects. You could help rig sound equipment for a local band or theater group. Most sound designers start as a runner or trainee, making coffee and loading gear.

GLOSSARY

acoustics The science of sound.

adaptor A device for connecting two parts of a device.

ADR Audio dialogue replacement.

attack The beginning of a sound.

bass The lower half of a musical tone range.

body The middle part of a sound where it is at its loudest.

boom A long more or less horizontal supporting arm or brace for holding a microphone.

boom operator The sound recordist who holds the boom.

decay The last part of a sound, as it fades away.

dialogue Conversation given in a written story or play.

director The person that guides the making of a movie or show.

director of photography The person who is in charge of filming for a movie.

dovetailing To fit or cause to fit together easily and conveniently.

echo The repeating of a sound caused by reflection of sound waves.

equalizers An electronic device (as in a sound-reproducing system) used to adjust response to different audio frequencies.

final mix The final version of a soundtrack.

Foley effects The reproduction of everyday sound effects that are added to a movie in post-production to enhance audio quality.

grip Part of the production team that builds and maintains all the equipment that supports cameras.

lavalier microphones A small microphone that is hung around the neck or clipped to the clothing of the user.

locations Places away from a studio where a movie is shot.

molecules A group of atoms bonded together, representing the smallest fundamental unit of a chemical compound that can take part in a chemical reaction.

pop shield A noise protection filter for microphones, that reduces or eliminates "popping" sounds caused by the mechanical impact of fast moving air.

post-production Work done on a film or recording after filming or recording has taken place.

room tone The "silence" recorded at a location or space when no dialogue is spoken.

royalty-free The right to use copyright material or intellectual property without needing to pay fees for each use.

shotgun microphones A highly directional microphone that must be pointed directly at its target sound source for proper recording.

showreel A short piece of footage containing examples of work for showing to potential employers.

sibilance Speech sound having a hissing effect.

software The programs and other operating information used by a computer.

sound mixer One that controls the volume and tone of sound picked up by microphones.

soundtrack A track (as on a movie or television videotape) that carries the sound record.

stimulate Encourage or arouse interest or enthusiasm in.

synchronize Cause to occur or operate at the same time or rate.

vibrations Continuous quick, slight shaking movements.

FOR MORE INFORMATION

Books

Bamford, Donna, and Farrell, Dan. *The Movie Making Book: Skills and Projects to Learn and Share*, Chicago, IL: Chicago Review Press, 2017.

Hynes, Patricia. *Sound Engineer (21st Century Skills Library: Cool Science Careers)*, North Mankato, MN: Cherry Lake Publishing, 2014.

Websites

Due to the changing nature of Internet links, PowerKids Press has developed an online list of websites related to the subject of this book. This site is updated regularly. Please use this link to access the list:

www.powerkidslinks.com/mm/sound

INDEX